# Girl...

*Tell Me Your Story*

## A GIFT OF POEMS
### FOR REFLECTION,
### CELEBRATION
### AND HEALING

# JACK GARNETT

# GIRL...TELL ME YOUR STORY
## A GIFT OF POEMS FOR REFLECTION, CELEBRATION AND HEALING

*iUniverse books may be ordered through booksellers or by contacting:*

*iUniverse*
*1663 Liberty Drive*
*Bloomington, IN 47403*
*www.iuniverse.com*
*1-800-Authors (1-800-288-4677)*

*ISBN: 978-1-4917-9217-9 (sc)*
*ISBN: 978-1-4917-9218-6 (e)*

*Print information available on the last page.*

*iUniverse rev. date: 04/16/2016*

# Foreword

As an avid traveler and educator, I have had the opportunity to meet and interact with various individuals from countries across the globe. The most intriguing stories, experiences and anecdotes that I have encountered are the ones from females.

Here, hopes, dreams, successes, failures, regrets, passions, tragedies, and triumphs, were conveyed with such unadulterated fervor, that upon reflection, I felt that in some way they are worth sharing. Thus, my thoughts began to center on how to bring these stories to life.

This book is a compilation of some of these stories being brought to life in the form of poetry. Although these poems are loosely based on actual events in the life of the woman/girl, they are imbued with a moderate sprinkling of my personal interpretation of what I have heard and seen. Included are elements drawn from North American and Europe; to the beautiful islands of the West Indies and the Great Pacific enclave. This book is certainly not intended for therapeutic use, but one for reflection, celebration, understanding and perhaps, healing.

Jack Garnett

# Table of Contents

# Trusting Innocence In My Hand

I was preparing to cut down all the plants in my
garden and prepare the soil for next Spring, when
I was blessed with a wonderful surprise.
You see, all my flowers had long died. I decided to
wait until the next day before I start weeding.

In the early morning I opened my front door
and something to the left of the fence,
in the thickness of the bush, caught my eye.
I quickly moved towards it to take a closer look.
To my surprise a single, fully developed red rose
stared innocently at me! A sweet miracle!

What is amazing about this find is that I pass the same spot every
day and never even knew that a rose bush existed there. And
just when I decided to chop the whole thing down.................

A message perhaps?

# Trusting Innocence In My Hand

## Reflections of the Heart

_____
_____
_____
_____
_____
_____
_____
_____
_____
_____
_____
_____
_____
_____
_____
_____
_____
_____
_____
_____
_____
_____
_____

# Don't Let The Night Take You

The dark night came upon me
My home I rushed to go
My car I started quickly
But little did I know

Money, money sir, a little hand tapped me softly
I swung around to look
A tiny frame stood before me
My heart sank and shook

Where did you come from my darling
Why do you have to be so poor
To take a chance and stop me
To knock on my car door

My heart broke to see you begging
With your long hair and tiny frame
So many men would try to use you
To make you their next game

Where is your mother here to guide you
Your father tall and brave
So anxious to protect you
Your little heart to save

# Don't Let The Night Take You

Go home my little one, go home
Your humble little bed calls for you
If the dark night should envelope you
My child of God, what would I do

Your face will always be before me
For the rest of my natural life
How from the dark you stopped me
And left me forever with pain and strife

# Don't Let The Night Take You

## Reflections of the Heart

# Hush, Hush, My Pain

Your hand so soft touched my pain
A mighty reassurance again and again
In spite of my resistance, pride and shame
You give me hope that your trust I will regain

You tell me words that I never knew
Complete and honest passion you shew
Content not just to talk but do
A high expression of faith so wonderful and true!

If someone had told me the way I would feel
Denial and accusation I would certainly reel
Such vision of grandeur that would heal
A moment with you that I could not help but steal

# Hush, Hush, My Pain

## Reflections of the Heart

# My Heart Hears

Come closer to my side
And tell me all your fears
A whispering you cannot hide
And I will feel your tears

To bathe me with such sorrow
Will increase my care for you
Confessions that removes the chill
And warms me through and through

Perhaps the time will pass away
When all is said and done
But you will always bless that day
When you became the one!

# My Heart Hears

## Reflections of the Heart

# A Little Girl's Dream

The little plane hovers overhead
My heart starts beating faster
I certainly know what my mind has said
But I refuse to make it my master

I saw him approach me and smile
Oh, he could be my salvation
But promises I have known for a while
So I held out no expectation

His kindness I refuse to receive
Although I am burning inside to accept it
Fearing those who make promises, then leave
Could this man's offering be legit

The two day visit passed so quickly
Joy and excitement filled the air
But though my schoolmates held onto him tightly
I could not let him know how much I care.

The little plane returned with a roar
Floating gently up into the sky
It took away the father I longed for
And all I can do is sit and cry!

# A Little Girl's Dream

## Reflections of the Heart

# Something Sweet!

I arrived at this lonely island retreat
A ragged maiden I would meet
Her question threw me off my feet
Did you bring me something sweet

I just picked out worms from my rice
I am dying for something nice
I am willing to pay the price
Forget my pride and roll the dice

Don't have shoes on my feet
Clean water and enough to eat
To you dear Sir, I do entreat
Open your bag and give me something sweet

I am sure you have some candy
Sweet bread or whatever you have handy
I am not into wine or brandy
Even a lollipop would be fine and dandy

Pain and sorrow have been my friend
My broken heart I need to mend
I cannot afford to break, so I bend
When will all the bad things end

It was now time for me to retreat
She clasp her hand and bowed at my feet
My heart just sank and skipped a beat
Please don't leave until you give me something sweet

# Something Sweet!

## Reflections of the Heart

# Refuse To Believe

My child, how much you purposely hurt me
Telling me all this, I can only say no
This thing so sad and cruel just cannot be
You're upsetting me and you will need to go

This intrusion will cause too much pain
You're taking my support from under my feet
The life that we now live will go down the drain
My duty and expenses I will not be able to meet

If I were to heed your cry and believe you
Pack his things, and demand that he had to leave
Think about your brother and sister, what will they do
Whose strength and support will they have to cleave

What's wrong with a man having a little bit of fun
They are wired a certain way and cannot change
It's not as if he was extremely rough and had a gun
Although he acted like a dog that's got mange

My heart is breaking as I think about this
Driving me mad and I no longer want to hear it
Gone are the days of living in ignorant bliss
My only advice to you … shut up and bear it

# Refuse To Believe

## Reflections of the Heart

# Too Much

Care too much
Bear too much
Give too much
Forgive too much

Save too much
Brave too much
Empathize too much
Sympathize too much

Say too much
Stay too much
Do too much
You too much

Hear too much
Dare too much
See too much
Agree too much

Hurt too much
Alert too much
Lose too much
Love too much

He gave you so much
Require from you much

# Too Much

## Reflections of the Heart

# Yuh Fehva Mi Fahda

Mi si yu a cum close
an mi naily jump outta mi seat
Mi caan figet di cussing mi get
an di ruff wey im dweet

Mi madda a cry inna night
an inna mawning look sadda
Mi tell yu, mi an di adda side af the ilan
but yu fehva mi fahda

Yu hack so kine,
you really cudda fool mi,
Dat yu ah gud sumaddi
an cudda tek care a mi

Finally a gud man dat wud put a
gal pickney life in aaahda
No sah mi can lowe mi self to tink dat
caaz yu fehva mi fahda

Noh laaf wid mi sah,
mi nah joke wid yu
If mi lowe yu too close,
mi no noe weh yu a go du

Pray fi mi massa,
dat noe outa hada
Al doe yu a mi pawsta yu fehva mi fahda

# Yuh Fehva Mi Fahda

## Reflections of the Heart

# What Else Could I Do

So what can you say boss,
do I get the job
You got what you wanted,
but my dignity you robbed

I have kept myself to myself,
never done anything like this
In fact, it wasn't until last month
that I had my first kiss

Why couldn't I get in
with my professional credentials?
I went to university and training school,
I have the essentials

I know these days life is hard
and there is nothing to do
I have a young gentleman in mind,
but certainly it wasn't you.

# What Else Could I Do

You told me this is
the only way to get ahead
Stop resisting so long,
time to live life, you said

I have school loans to pay,
my dear family expects me
To start earning my keep,
and be all I can be.

I will never forget
the great pain that you caused me
Not from the physical intrusion,
but my pride and security

My innocence is lost
and now inside I will continually sob
Welcome to the real world my dear,
all this for a lousy job!

# What Else Could I Do

## Reflections of the Heart

# The Need Inside!

Trapped deep inside is the me I cannot hide
So many things I must decide

To be raised from the ocean over the cruel tide
My deep longing you must not chide

I need the Savior by my side
For my sins he bled and died

The Holy Spirit as my guide
All my needs he will provide

God's tender mercies where' ere betide
From His strong arms I cannot slide

Above the clouds I will gloriously ride
My Heavenly home I will forever abide

# The Need Inside!

## Reflections of the Heart

_____
_____
_____
_____
_____
_____
_____
_____
_____
_____
_____
_____
_____
_____
_____
_____
_____
_____
_____
_____
_____
_____
_____
_____
_____
_____

# The Rose That Will Not Die!

I discovered you one day
as I ran through the door
Deep in the thicket filled with
rugged bush to the core

Your beauty and magnificence
immediately caught my eye
Didn't realize you would become
the rose that will not die

From the day that I saw you
in the forgotten garden
I would think by now
you'd be dull and your petal harden

But you remained nice and
sweet like a piece of pie
Your brilliance reminds me
of a rose that will not die

Your significance in warming hearts
is second to none
And your work in breaking down walls
is still not done

# The Rose That Will Not Die!

Giving hope to those whose
dreams have become a lie
Seems important that you
are the rose that will not die

"Trusting Innocence In My Hand"
is the fitting name
That I gave you when
that September morning came

Sweet kisses are expected
if you glow and not be shy
A well-deserved reward
for the rose that will not die

Winter comes soon
and snow will drop from the sky
To cover your presence
and cause the earth to cry

Then it will be time to shed a tear
as I say goodbye
Return to me next year,
beautiful rose that will not die

# The Rose That Will Not Die!

## Reflections of the Heart

# A Minute

Can I have a minute,
to tell you about my teacher
Listen to me a minute,
I don't need a preacher

Sit down with me a minute,
it won't take long
Spare me a minute,
let me know that I belong

Take a minute,
to show me that you really care
Talk with me a minute,
even if you need to go somewhere

I said a minute!!
Don't you understand what's in my heart?
I need a minute,
I can't stand always being apart

# A Minute

Share with me a minute,
I am tired of being alone
A simple minute,
your consistent attention I have never known

Wait a minute,
Don't get up and go
Just a minute,
There are so many things you don't know

Only a minute,
and I won't bother you no more
Give me a minute,
before you walk out that door

# A Minute

## Reflections of the Heart

# Look Mom.......Flowers!

Look Mom.....beautiful, wonderful flowers!
I think they have been sitting there for hours

Why not pick them up from behind the door
And why don't daddy come around any more

My darling I think you need to know
What he did and why he had to go

The bunch of roses that looks so sweet
He had used to sweep me off my feet

A morbid sense of overwhelming guilt
Just like the flower it will eventually wilt

Confessions have given him a temporary reprieve
But eventually he went too far, and had to leave

My broken heart he continue to pursue
But I have had enough, I wish he knew

A just reward for being up to no good
If only he was truthful and did what he should

My days are darker but you are my light
I hope that there will be no dream tonight

I will probably just sit and quietly cry for hours
And curse the day when he first brought me flowers

# Look Mom........Flowers!

Reflections of the Heart

# Sad To Say

So sorry again to say
There is no money or food today
Believe me, there is no other way
At home you must stay

Like a horse, resort to eating hay
No school with your girlfriend Kay
Begging again, this time I say nay
But we have each other comes what may

On top of that the sky is gray
We do suffer much more than they
Always trying to keep hunger at bay
As you moan and groan where you lay

There is no energy to go out and play
Learning opportunities disappearing day by day
Being poor, that is the price that we must pay
Have mercy on us O Heavenly Father, we pray!

# Sad To Say

## Reflections of the Heart

# Get Somebody Else!

Christmas time is coming along,
and I don't feel I am doing anything wrong,

To buy my children expensive gifts
that they don't really need

Look, I've got the money, and
you may think this is funny,

But I perceive it as getting into the true spirit
and performing my good deed

It's exceedingly unfair, to think that I don't really care
But I don't want to get caught up
into this never-ending cycle of compassion

Certainly, I have done some good,
as any other person would,
But my friends are successful and I must keep up by
sporting the latest fashion

As tempting as it might be,
to be responsible for some kid school fee,
No one wants to be engaged and locked
into a period of sustained commitment

What if my child needs a new phone,
one with the latest ring tone

# Get Somebody Else!

I simply have to oblige to avoid disrupting my feeling
of bliss and contentment

And then, there is going out to eat….
which for me is quite a necessary treat

My taste buds are tantalized
as I always go seconds and thirds on the punch

Focusing on this thing call charity,
in my circles is quite a rarity

We don't have the time to consider if some random
child don't have bus fare and lunch

So forget your appeal,
and with regards to sponsorship…..get real

A person's got to live it up and enjoy all the goods and
pleasures they manage to earn

Bother me no more
and your speeches …..I will ignore

Get somebody else to open a way and
give children Chances to learn

# Get Somebody Else!

## Reflections of the Heart

# For Some Reason

For some reason,
I don't feel the same way anymore

My back is still aching and my body is still sore
To block out this sadness is the task I must endure
Or it will drive me insane
and from that there's no cure

I will go for a long walk and not act like I am crazy
My eyes are filled with tears and my memory is a bit hazy

At least they will not say that I am rude and lazy
And I can drown my sorrow by picking a hibiscus or a daisy

An out of body experience
I will pretend this to be
A necessary evil
for an ambitious girl like me
To remain with people whose support I did
not see
I must fake it and smile,
which is something I cannot agree

# For Some Reason

You wear your skirt too short and draw too much attention
And you act like you are so special
and your voice is annoying, I forget to mention

You are always up front and your desire to lead
is beyond the normal convention
Yes, you are to blame
for a good man now in detention

For some reason,
I must not feel the same no more
I will never hope, love, and trust as I did before

I am not sure if I ever
want to walk back through that door
So I'll just keep going
far beyond this painful shore.

# For Some Reason

## Reflections of the Heart

# Finally, A Man In The House!

You don't know how hard
it is to be needy and alone
When the only time you connect
with him is by talking on the phone

So why be so judgemental;
who says he's going to be a louse
I am just happy that finally
there is going to be a man in the house.

You talk about being careful;
I should not do things in a hurry
That I'm a mother with a young girl,
but you don't need to worry

It's hard to spend so much of your time
looking for a spouse
Thank God Almighty there is
finally going to be a man in the house

# Finally, A Man In The House!

When you are older you will learn
That sometimes you have to close your eyes
To situations that you don't understand,
Even allowing him to tell some lies

So stop making up new stories,
why should he be as innocent as a mouse
You must learn to watch your tongue,
cause there is now a man in the house.

So my darling leave this one to me,
I've got everything under control
I am making the decisions here;
there is no need for heads to roll

If something starts to happen,
there's no fire I can't douse
Calm down and take it easy,
my red-blooded man is in the house!

# Finally, A Man In The House!

## Reflections of the Heart

_____

_____

_____

_____

_____

_____

_____

_____

_____

_____

_____

_____

_____

_____

_____

_____

_____

_____

_____

_____

_____

_____

_____

_____

# I Need To Know

I heard you crying on the phone last night
And wondering if everything is alright
I need to know!

Is your professor very kind
Or is he corrupting your mind
I need to know!

You're so far away,
Have you forgotten how to pray
I need to know!

Do you still struggle with pride
Your contempt for the ordinary you can't hide
I need to know!

Is the location of the next party your point of reference
Whether something is good or bad, can you still tell the difference
I need to know!

Considering all the varied avenues of deception
Can you determine which concept you should give reception
I need to know!

# I Need To Know

With all the pressure coming from your new peers
Would you consider returning to base to relieve all my fears
I need to know!

Will you be careful in what you do with your body
Can we depend on your determination to remain somebody
I need to know!

You know what they say, how the world was created
Would you stand your ground when this topic is debated
I need to know!

Money, fashion and fame will soon pass away
Will you purpose in your heart to live for Him day by day
I need to know!

Your family and church is depending on you
To consider these questions,
to use wisdom in what you choose to do
Our confidence in your abilities is second to none
Surely your success will be guaranteed as
long as you stay close to The One!
This I do know!

# I Need To Know

## Reflections of the Heart

# I See You

I see you…..when you hid as I passed by
You caused me to shiver and I really don't know why
Considering you are never here to tuck me in
My emotions are dead through thick and thin

I know you…...really don't care for me
Your actions speak loudly and your words are empty
Who is it that is getting all your attention?
And your hugs are so insincere, I forgot to mention

I feel you…...have other things on your mind
The love you have is always looking behind
Just stay for a moment, this is not a game
I would not be surprised if you have forgotten my name

I hate you…and I feel ashamed to say
That such strong emotion could ever come my way
This little girl's heart is hurting so bad
I regret the day when I first called you dad!

# I See You

## Reflections of the Heart

_____
_____
_____
_____
_____
_____
_____
_____
_____
_____
_____
_____
_____
_____
_____
_____
_____
_____
_____
_____
_____
_____
_____
_____
_____
_____

# Waiting For My Shoes

Here I stand, so grand,
in my beautiful dress
There is certainly
no time to lose
My excitement is great,
so hard to suppress
I am waiting for
my man to bring shoes

He went far away
with promises sweet
This gift for my own I did choose
When he returns, oh…..
we will certainly meet
My dream to be graced with new shoes

Not constrained by time,
I 'm a young lady now
My life seem confined just to cruise
Walking bare feet,
I must change that somehow
How dignified I would look with new shoes

# Waiting For My Shoes

A poor island girl must
sometimes wait for a man
Who has not been
held captive by booze
His promises I will hold,
just as long as I can
And fantasize about
strutting in fine shoes

Sometimes I lose hope,
four months have already gone
I am tempted to think
t'was a ruse
For I gave him my love
and stayed until dawn
All for the comfort
of sporting new shoes

Yes, this wonderful dress,
seems incomplete with bare feet
And my badly worn toes
start to ooze
But I will hold my head high,
no need to retreat
My God will answer the
call for new shoes

# Waiting For My Shoes

## Reflections of the Heart

# Do You Think I Care?

Do you think I care that again
you can't face the day
And for constant deliverance
you so desperately pray
The confessions that you hope
will bring you peace
From the depth of sorrow
your longing heart will cease?

So many growling,
pathetic little stomachs around you
Just send them off
and hope someone will come through
Nothing will satisfy the insidious pain that took residence inside
You have shed enough tears
and your sorrow you can no longer hide

# Do You Think I Care?

The goals that you envision
and continue to foolishly set
Are certainly naive and will not anytime soon be met
A figment of your fantasy- engaged,
miss- directed imagination
Are reserved for those
who dabble in provocative sensation

Those who on your sustenance and protection depend
Will soon understand that their faith and trust must come to an end
Their future outside the home they must undesirably seek
Even though they are so young,
impressionable, and so sadly meek

No one cares, and this is not surprisingly true
I am in the same depressive boat as you
Thus when you reconcile that in your pretty head
Hopefully your dreams are not already dead!

# Do You Think I Care?

## Reflections of the Heart

# A Painful Choice

I trembled with fear
as the tall man approached me
My knees knock uncontrollably
but what else could I do
With courage mixed with shame
I must resist the urge to flee
My future lies in my will
to hold on and see this through

My book-list in hand,
I held onto my girlfriend
She often boasts about her time on the street
"That one seem to like you, your night will not end
Until I show you some like him that you need to meet"

"Young girl you are so pretty and I
am so surprised you are here
But truth be told, I am happy
that my night will be exciting and fun
What's the price you are charging
I hope you are not too dear"
"Oh, One thousand or 10 dollars US";
my lips trembled and I wanted to run.

# A Painful Choice

My head want to explode,
as I remember the early summer
When I asked family, friends, church members,
anyone; to help me
I want to serve my country and community;
I am not a newcomer
So much for that, no one was prepared
to answer my plaintiff plea

The alternative is heartbreaking;
I can't stay home and do nothing
The boredom alone will certainly take my life
Many talk about my potential;
that I will amount to something
So I have chosen this uncertain path loaded with more pain and strife

He pulled me to his vehicle;
I reluctantly follow
O God, what is this crazy thing
I am about to do
This time if I scream,
it will be so uselessly hallow
I shudder at the possible sense of loss that will ensue

# A Painful Choice

"Please don't hurt me sir,
believe me it's my first time".
My throat was so tight;
I could scarcely hear my voice

"Just shut up and say nothing,
your time is now mine
You did what you had to,
this is your choice".

"People today are conveniently
wrapped up in selfishness and greed
They would care less about a girl
that can't afford to go to school.
As sick as it sounds,
what I am doing to you is my good deed
This experience will help change your life
from ordinary to cool".

I have never known a real father,
he could be my daddy
How often I dreamt of that time
When a strong man would protect me,
treat me like a princess
But now I know that lot will never be mine

# A Painful Choice

I closed my eyes so tightly,
my head spun and nearly burst with pain
Never thought I would end up in this position;
not the way it ought to be
"Hey gal, you still has a future; tonight you have made so much gain
Don't forget your list; you've earned your
money for books and school fee".

I ran back to my girlfriend,
tears of great loss I could not hide
She is more hardened by life,
having succumbed to coercion and favor
No longer feeling like a child,
I must stand with my peers side by side
With so many pretenders,
will someone lead me to find The True Saviour?

# A Painful Choice

## Reflections of the Heart

# Please Don't Send Me Away

I stood silently before him, my eyes fixated to the floor
"Show yourself to the Priest", one shouted,
as I walked through the door
My body ached as I entered, Lord, forgive all my sins I pray
And touch the heart of this kind man with
the power to send me away

Her hands were covered with sores, her feet and body too
How much she must have suffered, but did not know what to do
The decision I must make here, is packed with multiple shades of gray
It's not like she is that important, why shouldn't I send her away

You haven't paid your school fees, you shouldn't even be here
Educational and other responsibilities, certainly your cross to bear
Your classmates tease and scorn you, beside them you cannot stay
I am saving you the embarrassment, if I choose to send you away

# Please Don't Send Me Away

I came first in my class and my teacher says I am tremendously gifted
Somehow I feel that counts for something
and my spirit has been lifted
I was so happy and hopeful this morning,
now my joy has turned to dismay
Just give me a little spot in the corner, but please don't send me away

She bowed her head in anguish, tugged at her skin and began to cry
Kind Sir, are you without compassion, do you want to watch me die
Without the safety and security of this place,
keeping the evil world at bay
Dear God, my heart would be broken, if you decide to send me away

You have become my family, a caring protector I never had
So much suffering I've encountered and my luck is always bad
I never knew my feeble, thirsting soul would see the light of day
Even though I'm a dirty outcast, cancel sending me away

# Please Don't Send Me Away

I was beginning to feel like somebody,
knowing I am a part of your school
But now I fear that I am being considered
a nobody and an unrealistic fool
My life and future is in your hand, there is not much more I can say
I will be totally devastated, with a decision to send me away

I looked at her in silence; grieving hearts is hard to take
But I must be practical in my dealings,
and decisions I choose to make
She is just one rejected person, that's the price she must now pay
The majority rules this enclave; they would agree to send her away

Leave the school this hour; lead this poor soul through the gate
Somehow I hope she will forgive us and her
heart will not be filled with hate
"Unclean, Unclean" I declare you; plead and beg as you may
Perhaps I will call for you in the future, it's
decided; I must send you away!

# Please Don't Send Me Away

## Reflections of the Heart

_____
_____
_____
_____
_____
_____
_____
_____
_____
_____
_____
_____
_____
_____
_____
_____
_____
_____
_____
_____
_____
_____
_____
_____
_____

# You Can Sleep Tonight

Hiding my sister in a barrel,
I crouch beneath my bed at night
It seems somewhere this wouldn't be normal,
to be petrified with fright
They are here again to disturb our innocence;
Tears and pain before daylight
Could it be that out there, anywhere;
Children are having peaceful sleep tonight?

Does it matter how we got here;
Poverty cause our parents to take flight
Leaving three girls in a house
with no food, diminished hope, and no light
Unprotected from wicked elements;
Something here is certainly not right
Isn't it nice and beautiful to know,
you will experience sweet sleep tonight?

Going to school is out of the question
Would you even consider giving me a single mite
When you hear that I haven't eaten all day
and my needs are out of sight
Really now, a poverty stricken girl;
Condemned never to reach the proverbial height
Will a nobody like me even cross your mind
as you enjoy wonderful sleep tonight?

# You Can Sleep Tonight

I have nothing to offer;
From my emptiness society has taken a cruel bite
Would it be a fair exchange if I give you my body;
And you just consider my plight?
Maybe it's time to throw in the towel,
To keep my dignity I will no longer fight
Oh, let me continue to dodge the merciless intruder;
While you relax and sleep tonight

Sadness reigns with me and my sisters
As we hold each other tight
In this hopeless place so dark and dingy
Where non-stop evil is here to spite
We must survive and come to something;
Or die trying with all our might
Will you consider helping us distant stranger;
As you tenderly sleep right through the night!

# You Can Sleep Tonight

## Reflections of the Heart

_____
_____
_____
_____
_____
_____
_____
_____
_____
_____
_____
_____
_____
_____
_____
_____
_____
_____
_____
_____
_____
_____
_____
_____
_____
_____

Printed in the United States
By Bookmasters